Original title:
A Walk in Paradise

Copyright © 2025 Creative Arts Management OÜ
All rights reserved.

Author: Miriam Kensington
ISBN HARDBACK: 978-1-80581-515-0
ISBN PAPERBACK: 978-1-80581-042-1
ISBN EBOOK: 978-1-80581-515-0

Beneath the Veil of Vibrant Ferns

In ferns so bright, I lost my shoe,
A squirrel laughed, said, "What's wrong with you?"
The leaves they danced, a wobbly show,
I joined their jig, with my toe in tow.

A toad croaked tunes, a poet at heart,
He waved his arms, said, "Let's make art!"
With every step, my pants did tear,
I giggled loud, forgot my care.

Footprints on Soft Paradisiacal Sands

Sandy trails beneath my goofy feet,
Seagulls squawked, made the beach a treat.
I built a tower, it fell with a splat,
The tide came in, 'There's my welcome mat!'

With each new splash, a shriek of glee,
A crab waved back, just as sly as me.
My hat took flight, a seagull's goal,
It landed aim-high on a sunbather's soul.

Kaleidoscope of Nature's Serenade

Butterflies fluttered, with wings that shine,
They danced around, making me pine.
I chased a bee, it was quite absurd,
And ended up tangled in floral curds.

The daisies laughed as I tumbled through,
With colors bright, a vibrant view.
I posed for selfies with my new bug friends,
Who knew nature's giggles would never end?

Eden's Embrace in Every Step

With every step, I slipped on leaves,
A tree said, "Careful! You're such a tease!"
The flowers winked, their petals bright,
A parade of petals, what a crazy sight!

I pranced around like a quirky sprite,
Grinning at clouds, all fluffy and white.
A rainbow appeared, said, "Join the fun!"
I twirled and laughed, 'til the day was done.

Gliding Through Blossom-Scented Air

Wobbly bees in the breeze,
Chasing dreams on sticky knees,
Tulips giggle, daisies pout,
Who knew flowers could shout?

Socks with sandals, what a sight,
Dancing with worms, pure delight,
Dandelions laugh, roots in glee,
Oh, the joy of being free!

The Garden of Endless Horizons

Gnomes are plotting, plain as day,
Trading hats for a grand ballet,
Rabbits hopping with flair and spin,
Who'll take the crown? Let the games begin!

Sunflowers gossip, turning heads,
While grasshoppers jump on their beds,
Chasing ants in a wild chase,
Nature's circus—a merry place!

Radiance in Each Gentle Step

With every step, the clouds giggle,
Tickling toes that jump and wiggle,
Squirrels stare with puzzled frowns,
At silly hats and mismatched crowns.

Butterflies prance in fluffy shoes,
Pollen parties—who could refuse?
Laughter echoes through the trees,
Nature's humor, sure to please!

Amongst the Golden Petals

Doves dressed up in fancy wear,
Sipping nectar without a care,
Sunset rays doing a sun dance,
While rabbits strut in a bold prance.

A caterpillar sings a tune,
To baker bees who bake by noon,
Fluffy clouds play tag up high,
As rainbows join, oh me, oh my!

Vistas of Unspoken Dreams

In fields where daisies dance and prance,
A goat in boots joins the merry chance.
It plays the tune of joyful glee,
As chickens cha-cha by the old cedar tree.

Clouds wear hats made of cotton fluff,
While squirrels juggle acorns, sure enough!
A rainbow slips on roller skates,
And laughter echoes 'round the garden gates.

Envisioning Harmonious Realms

A frog in shades croaks out a song,
He sways by the pond, where critters belong.
Ladybugs groove in a dance so bright,
While bumblebees buzz in sheer delight.

Ducks quack chorus to a sunbeam's call,
And flowers giggle, oh, they've seen it all!
A breeze tickles noses, as petals sway,
In this realm, silliness leads the way.

Tranquil Moments Under Ancient Trees

Beneath a tree with a squawky crow,
A picnic ensues with snacks on tow.
Ants in tuxedos march on the sheet,
While worms perform jazz with wiggly beat.

Leaves whisper secrets in a gossip spree,
"Did you see the squirrel steal a grandpa's tea?"
The roots are comfy, like nature's couch,
As butterflies burst into a colorful ouch!

Reflections of Joy on the Trail

On the path where giggles bloom so bright,
A turtle taxis under a starry night.
Wide-eyed rabbits play hopscotch and chase,
While clouds toss confetti, just to embrace.

Raccoons wear moon hats, all fluff and cheer,
They toast to the sunset with bottles of beer.
With each silly step, the world seems to spin,
In this joyful journey, let the fun begin!

Horizons that Whisper Secrets

In a land where the clouds play,
I tripped on a unicorn's ray.
It winked at me with a grin,
As I stumbled into a bin.

The flowers giggled in cheer,
As I danced with an old, fluffy deer.
We held a tea party with bees,
They spilled honey on my knees.

I heard the mountains chuckle low,
As I fell for a slippery show.
A rainbow slide, just my luck,
Into a puddle—oh, what muck!

But joy's in the clumsy, you'll find,
With laughter that brightens the mind.
So skip through this whimsical spree,
Where secrets and fun run free!

Songs of the Skybound Wanderer

Up above, a bird starts to croon,
I stepped on a worm—what a swoon!
He looked up and gave me a frown,
As I wobbled and danced like a clown.

The clouds gathered for a silly show,
With jokes that only they know.
A sunbeam tickled my nose,
And I laughed till I struck a pose.

A butterfly flew in a whirl,
And tied my shoelace in a curl.
I chased him, but ended in mud,
And found a flower that sang—I bud!

So roam with the winds that play,
In this world, bright and gay.
Where songs of delight never tire,
And whimsical laughter climbs higher!

Interludes in a Lavender Dream

In fields of violet, I twirled,
Till I found a snail that swirled.
He wore a hat, so chic and blue,
And said, "Join me, let's glide through!"

We raced under the skies so clear,
With laughter louder than a cheer.
But oh, he stopped to take a nap,
While I slipped on a daisies' flap!

A butterfly burst into a spin,
Amusingly mocking my little win.
"Your shoes are muddy!" it teased with glee,
As I joined in a dance with a bee.

So here in this lavender hue,
With giggles and silliness, fun ensues.
Embrace the dance, embrace the gleam,
And let your thoughts flow in a dream!

Luminous Pathways Through the Verdant Realm

I wandered through paths all aglow,
Stepped on a rake—Oh, what a show!
It flapped up, a slap on my face,
As I tumbled down in disgrace.

The trees chimed in with a laugh,
While squirrels plotted their next crafty half.
A hedgehog winked, then rolled away,
While I sprawled out in bushes' sway.

Oh, the mushrooms danced in a ring,
Inviting me in for a silly fling.
But I slipped on a vine (what a trap!),
And landed right in a toad's lap!

Yet here in the twinkling green sights,
Where joy leaps with silly flights.
Find your laughter, let it prevail,
On this luminous, funny trail!

Wandering through Star-Kissed Gardens

In gardens where the daisies dance,
I tripped on roses, lost my pants.
The lilies giggled, swayed with glee,
While bees buzzed tunes just for me.

The moonlight shone on rubber ducks,
As squirrels played pranks, oh what luck!
I chased a butterfly on a whim,
And ended up in water, quite grim.

The geraniums whispered cheeky tales,
Of garden gnomes with crooked nails.
They winked at me through leaves so bright,
While I pondered the wrongs of my flight.

With laughter echoing through the night,
I found my way with giggles alight.
These star-kissed paths, a silly spree,
Where all's a jest, and I'm lost in glee.

The Symphony of Sun and Bloom

In fields of sun, the flowers sway,
While I attempted cartwheels today.
The daisies clapped, the sunflowers smiled,
As I tumbled like a clumsy child.

A breeze took my hat, it flew so high,
I waved goodbye and let out a sigh.
The sun played tricks, peeked through the trees,
While butterflies tagged me with ease.

The woof of a pup caught my delight,
As he pranced around, what a silly sight.
Dandelions puffed with giddy cheer,
As I chased them down, oblivious to fear.

With petals strewn and laughter loud,
I joined the flowers, feeling proud.
In sunlight's grip, I danced all day,
Creating my own bouquet of play.

Beyond the Gates of Radiant Daydreams

I wandered past the wobbly gate,
Where dewdrops served a wobbly plate.
The clouds rumbled, but not from rain,
Just giggles bursting like a train!

Rabbits in tuxedos bowed with flair,
Chasing my thoughts like they didn't care.
The sun threw confetti, bright and bold,
While squirrels juggled acorns, uncontrolled!

In this land where dreams collide,
I found a lion who wanted to hide.
He wore a mask, oh what a scene,
Claiming he's shy, but oh so keen!

As shadows danced under candy trees,
I laughed so hard, I fell to my knees.
In daydreams where silliness reigns supreme,
Life's just a happy, twisted dream.

Whispers of Eden

In whispers soft, the flowers chuckle,
As I mistook a butterfly for a buckle.
The carrots giggled, the tomatoes blushed,
When a rain cloud came along and rushed.

A parrot squawked, "What do you dare?"
As I stumbled past without a care.
Banana peels lay waiting for me,
While daisies clapped in sheer harmony.

With cherries singing and grapes at play,
The fruit parade rolled right my way.
I tried to salsa through the vine,
And ended up tangled, oh how divine!

Through whispers sweet and jests so light,
I reveled in this garden's delight.
In Eden's reach, all became clear,
Life's better with laughter and a cheer.

Revelations in the Blossom Bower

In a bower thick with blooms,
Bees dance in silly costumes.
Butterflies tease old man's hat,
While a squirrel steals his snack.

Tulips gossip, wine glasses clink,
While daisies mull and delicately wink.
A rabbit hops with an air of pride,
Claiming the throne where daisies abide.

The sun throws seeds of playful light,
As petals giggle, taking flight.
Laughter mingles with the breeze,
Nature's jesters, delightfully tease.

In this realm of joy and cheer,
Even the worms shed a tear.
For in this fun-filled, fragrant show,
Every creature laughs, no room for woe.

Footfalls in the Garden of Dreams

Footfalls echo on the path,
Where tulips conduct a floral bath.
Worms wriggle as the crows strut,
While daisies offer free donuts.

Barking flowers with bloated cheeks,
Critique the fashion of the creeks.
Grasshoppers jump, like they own the place,
Clueless to the frogs ready to race.

A wise old crow rants about bills,
While ladybugs share their fortune spills.
Matters of love with petals create,
In this dreamscape, all is first-rate.

Beneath the sun, ridiculous pranks,
The trees all giggle and form little swanks.
Every step in this wilful scheme,
Is a giggle shared in a garden dream.

A Symphony of Sunbeams

Sunbeams dance like giddy sprites,
Tickling flowers, delighting sights.
The daisies tap their flowery toes,
Disco vibes as the sunlight glows.

A bumblebee with swagger and flair,
Buzzes around, too cool to care.
Flowers gossip with awkward grace,
Trying to keep up in the sunny race.

A pet cat licks its fluffy paw,
Then chases shadows, an enormous flaw.
Sunlight's warmth, it takes a nap,
Dreaming of mischief with a purring clap.

In this absurd series of beams,
Reality bends, or so it seems.
A garden stage, where all partake,
In the playful song of nature's wake.

Embracing Nature's Elation

With arms wide open, plants all cheer,
Singing songs to the giggling deer.
The trees chuckle, leaves a-flutter,
Over a toad's poetic utter.

Bouncing bunnies on pogo sticks,
Form a band with clever tricks.
Marigolds wear polka dot hats,
As the gardener scolds the gossiping cats.

Frogs breakdance on lily pads,
While tadpoles cheer with joyful jads.
A playful wind joins the fray,
Swooping low like a child at play.

In this realm of joyful grace,
Every frown finds a cozy place.
Nature's elation, a humorous twist,
One big laugh; oh, how we persist!

Glimpses of the Infinite Blossom

In gardens where the daisies chat,
The tulips toss their hats, just like a cat.
Butterflies with giggles flutter high,
As bees play tag beneath the azure sky.

A peacock struts, a fashion show in bloom,
While squirrels gossip by the mushroom room.
The clouds are fluffy, soft as whipped cream,
And in this chaos, we all twist and scream.

A cactus cracks jokes, oh what a sight,
Telling puns under the moonlight bright.
The roses blush in a silly brawl,
While sunflowers try their best to stand tall.

Laughter erupts as the daisies dance,
And frogs in tuxedos take a chance.
What a place to prance and play,
Where silliness blooms every day!

Pathways to the Celestial Heart

On paths where dandelions shout hooray,
And rabbits race on a sunny day.
An owl in glasses reads a map,
While turtles wear hats - oh, what a flap!

The breeze whispers jokes with a twist,
As flowers join in, they cannot resist.
A leaf tumbles down with a giggly swish,
Pond frogs chant, 'Oh, grant us a wish!'

In this enchanted, wacky land,
Even the stones have a helping hand.
As sunset giggles in vibrant hues,
The stars appear, all wearing their shoes!

Laughter flows like a bubbling brook,
In every nook, a playful hook.
This trail leads to joy, oh what a start,
On the pathways to the celestial heart!

Dancing Petals in a Gentle Breeze

Petals pirouette in a vibrant show,
Under the gaze of the sun's soft glow.
A squirrel attempts a ballet leap,
While all around, the flowers peep.

The breeze whispers secrets, oh how they tease,
With giggles and chuckles swirling with ease.
In this floral dance, the laughter flows,
As daisies tell jokes nobody knows.

Butterflies giggle and twirl on a whim,
While glowing fireflies start to swim.
The whole meadow joins in, oh what a sight,
Laughter under stars, everything feels right.

With every rustle and every hum,
Nature's chorus sings along, here we come!
In these antics, joy's the one we please,
Dancing petals in a gentle breeze.

Aromas of Serenity

In fields where the lavender takes a bow,
The daisies chuckle, 'Can you smell it now?'
With scents so sweet they make you grin,
Even the grumpy snails rush in.

Aromatic laughter fills the air,
As bees concoct potions of sweet flair.
The garden gnomes whisper secrets loud,
And cover their ears when the sun's too proud.

Amidst the herb riot, a minty jest,
Where thyme and basil put friendship to the test.
The sunflowers laugh, their heads held high,
As ladybugs march with a cheerful sigh.

In this fragrant world, where whimsy reigns,
Every whiff brings joy across the plains.
In aromas of serenity, find your delight,
Where even the night seems giggly and bright!

Fantasia of Flora

In a garden where daisies smile,
The squirrels dance in cotton style.
Bees wear tiny hats and bow,
While the flowers giggle, "Oh wow!"

Breezes tickle the tulips' toes,
Petals play peek-a-boo, I suppose.
Ladybugs wear polka dot suits,
And the grass plays tunes on tree roots.

Worms in top hats wiggle and twirl,
While butterflies flaunt a dainty whirl.
A gnome attempts a grand pirouette,
But lands in a pot, you won't forget!

In this realm of frisky delight,
Where mushrooms glow soft in the night.
Chuckle and frolic, lose your cares,
Embrace the whimsy found in layers.

Sunlit Trails of Wonder

Under branches, shadows dance,
Bunnies join a loving prance.
Chasing sunbeams on the run,
Each moment filled with silly fun.

Birds don sunglasses, oh so cool,
Sipping nectar from a pool.
An owl snickers from a tree,
"What a sight, just look at me!"

Lizards in bowties stutter and slide,
While frogs in tuxedos take a ride.
A picnic blanket tops the hill,
Where ants train hard for their next thrill!

Giggles echo through the glade,
As nature throws a big parade.
So come along, don't be shy,
In this sunny kingdom, let's fly high!

A Sojourn in Joy

Strolling on clouds, fluffy and white,
Tickled by rainbows, what a sight.
Laughter echoes, bunnies cheer,
As we skip through fields, full of cheer.

Cats on skateboards race with flair,
Juggling fish while soaring in air.
A snail in shades takes a bold leap,
While giggling daisies dance, no sleep!

Cotton candy trees sway with sass,
While elephants dance like they're in class.
Giggly fairies stir sweet delight,
Painting the sky with colors bright.

Join the fun, come take a spin,
In this place where joy's our kin.
Life's too short for a heavy sigh,
Let's laugh and twirl as days go by!

Echoes of the Faerie Glen

In a glen where dreams run free,
Faeries giggle under a tree.
With wings that sparkle, they play tag,
While a raccoon attempts a brag.

Mice in shoes tap-dance with glee,
As a sheep in pajamas counts to three.
Gnarled trees chuckle with the breeze,
Swapping tales with such great ease.

A bear with glasses reads a book,
While mushrooms form a secret nook.
Rocking chairs made from willow twine,
Bring laughter, joy, and endless rhyme.

Every step feels light and bright,
In this enchanted realm of delight.
So grab your friends, come join the scene,
In the faerie glen, so fresh and green!

Ethereal Echoes Under the Moon

In a night so bright, we tripped on stars,
Chasing shadows of the cute little cars.
Laughter echoed, a sound like bells,
As we danced with the breeze and rang our own swells.

We stumbled on pixies, their wings all aglow,
They giggled and whispered, 'Oh no, no, no!'
With a wink and a flick, they zipped through the night,
Leaving us chuckling at their playful flight.

The moon was our spotlight, shining so clear,
We argued with frogs about who had the cheer.
They croaked for a chorus, we clapped in delight,
Our impromptu concert lasted till light.

As dawn started creeping, we yawned and we sighed,
What a fantastical journey, we'll carry with pride.
With eyes full of glee, we bid the night adieu,
Dreaming of echoes, where the laughter just grew.

Twilight Serenade of the Blossoms

Beneath the sky's canvas, we whirled 'round a tree,
A branch hung low, and it whispered to me,
'The flowers are singing, catch the bee's refrain,'
But we fell in the puddle, laughing hard after pain.

Petals pirouetted, adorned our hair,
Bees buzzed around us, unaware of the flair.
The tomatoes turned red, unsure what to do,
As we danced on the grass, all covered in dew.

With giggles like raindrops and a skip in our feet,
We serenaded blooms, a whimsical treat.
An orchestra of nature led us to cheer,
While squirrels looked puzzled; were we weird, or dear?

The twilight was sparkling, our smiles agleam,
Nature clapped loudly, or was it a dream?
Whichever it was, we cared not a stitch,
In a world full of wonders, we relished the glitch.

Converging Paths of Joy

Two trails diverged, one led to a cake,
But the other was shy, a path that would quake.
So hand in hand, we dove down the way,
To a land of giggles and rare cabaret.

With cupcakes that sang and a river of cheese,
We wobbled and whimpered, but never a freeze.
The path twisted gently, with whispers and grins,
As we picked up the humor, wore life's silly skins.

We played tag with the daisies, catching their laugh,
But they tickled us back with their flowery craft.
Then we tumbled in clover, a patch soft and wide,
Rolling 'round like tumbleweeds, head over stride.

At the junction of joy, where the butterflies dart,
With each silly choice, we stole beats from the heart.
No maps needed here, each twist was a gift,
In life's funny circus, the spirits would lift.

Luminous Strewn Petals

Sprinkled like confetti, the petals so bright,
They led us to giggles, in the warm, sunny light.
But wait! There's a gopher who thinks he can race,
And with a quick hop, he's now in our space!

We followed the giggles, though not on the path,
Through a forest of chuckles and vibrant math.
Numbers danced round us, one plus one equals two,
But add a few giggles, and three becomes you!

With whispers of secrets in the trembling leaves,
We knew every mischief, together, achieves.
Chasing the sunlight and the butterflies' flights,
Filling our pockets with laughter and sights.

As petals kept falling, we skipped side by side,
In a world full of color, we joyously glide.
So here's to the moments, as bliss waves parade,
In a garden of humor, our memories are made.

Strolling Through Heavenly Fields

Beneath the sun, I skip along,
Chasing clouds with a painted song.
Butterflies giggle as they flit,
While daisies in the breeze just sit.

A squirrel with shades, what a sight!
Dancing shadows, pure delight.
I bump into a cheeky bee,
Who buzzes, laughing, 'Come and see!'

Pigeons in tuxedos strut,
Critiquing all the scenes they cut.
I join their ranks, a dapper fool,
Lost in this absurdity, my rule.

The grass whispers jokes, quite absurd,
As frogs recite lines, slightly blurred.
With every step, I trip and slide,
In this playful realm, I glide.

Footprints in Celestial Meadows

In fields where laughter rules the day,
I leave behind my socks of gray.
Mice in sneakers race for crumbs,
While flowers dance to silly drums.

Upon clouds, I bounce and sway,
Frolicking with a cow on holiday.
A rabbit with a quirky hat,
Tells me secrets about the cat.

Silly petals tickle my nose,
As musical grass grows in rows.
I step on ladybugs, oh dear!
Yet they just chuckle, never fear.

In this paradise of woo and laugh,
Even the wind takes the wacky path.
Drawing smiley faces in the mist,
Making memories that can't be missed.

Pathways of Bliss

Wandering paths where picnic ants roam,
I zigzag about in my flowery dome.
The sun winks as I twist and twirl,
With daisies plotting a mischievous whirl.

Clouds play poker; it's quite the game,
While I ponder if it's autumn or fame.
Hiccups of laughter roll in the grass,
As squirrels critique my funky class.

The meadows blush in hues of fun,
Every step is a whacky pun.
I tried to skip but tripped on air,
The daisies giggled, "You're quite the pair!"

A walrus slides down a rainbow tail,
While unicorns munch on jelly pails.
Frolicking joy, this comedy spree,
I'm stuck here forever, at least, that's the key!

Dreams Beneath the Canopy

Underneath leafy dreams I prance,
With gophers joining this dance of chance.
The sun plays peek-a-boo up high,
While I attempt to fly, oh my!

But with my luck, I hit a branch,
The birds laugh loud, it's quite the chance.
"Come join the fun," a chipmunk shouts,
As laughter echoes in joyful bouts.

Sweet fruits drop like confetti rain,
While grasshoppers serenade my pain.
Each tiny step's a hefty jest,
In this realm of silliness, I'm blessed.

I roll down hills in syrupy glee,
Chasing giggles, forever carefree.
And as I pause to catch my breath,
I find in humor, there's no death!

Flowing Streams of Eternal Laughter

By the bubbling brook, I trip and slide,
Fish giggle loudly, oh what a ride!
My shoes are soggy, but spirits are high,
As ducks quack jokes, oh me, oh my!

Butterflies dance in a clumsy show,
Whispering secrets as breezes blow.
I wave at a tree, it waves back at me,
Are we friends now? Oh, glee and glee!

Clouds take shapes of a laughing clown,
Tickling the sun, making him frown.
"Keep it down!" he shouts, but we can't help it,
Laughter erupts, we're all in the pit!

Together we tumble down this bright trail,
With giggles and chuckles like a circus sale.
This paradise blooms with joy all around,
In flowing streams where laughter is found.

The Blooming Path to Elysium

Petunias pirouette, daisies take flight,
Bumblebees buzzing, a silly sight.
I'm lost in a field of giggly delight,
Where smiles bloom bright like stars in the night.

A squirrel recounts his wildest tale,
About nuts and mischief without fail.
His fluffy tail tickles my nose,
I laugh so hard, a real comedy prose!

Sunflowers nodding, agreeing with glee,
They gossip in whispers just like me.
Each step is a dance, every glance a grin,
In this blooming path, how can we not win?

With petals that flutter in playful cheer,
Nature's jester shows no fear.
Every moment here feels so divine,
As I skip down this path, oh how we shine!

Daydreams in Nature's Refuge

Under wide skies, I lay on the grass,
Watching shapes change, passing clouds flash.
A frog croaks jokes, with comedic flair,
Dancing with daisies, without a care!

Bees make a buzz, like tiny drummers,
Marching in sync, creating sweet murmurs.
I join their parade, with a jiggly jig,
Feeling so small, like a fruit in a fig!

Crickets serenade with their night-time tunes,
While owls hoot stories beneath the moons.
Daydreams abound with curiosity,
In this refuge of laughter, wild and free.

With every stitch of grass, I find delight,
Nature winks at me, oh what a sight!
In this whimsical land, I'm never alone,
For even the rocks, they chuckle and groan.

Cherished Steps in Sacred Spaces

Each step I take feels like a dance,
In sacred spaces, I take a chance.
A pebble rolls, like it has a mind,
Stumbling me gently, it's so unkind!

Laughter erupts from a tree branch above,
As squirrels debate who's the best at love.
They fluff their tails with exaggerated pride,
All while I'm chuckling, taking it in stride!

The sun winks at me, with rays like gold,
Tickling my skin, oh, nature's bold!
With flowers that chuckle and grass that sways,
I feel so alive in these comical ways.

In cherished steps, I roam this mirth,
A playground of joy, a patch of earth.
With laughter my guide, I explore with bliss,
In these sacred spaces, I find my kiss.

Secrets of the Enchanted Path

In the woods, the squirrels plot,
Wearing tiny hats, they dance a lot.
Mushrooms giggle, as they glow,
While rabbits play tag, stealing the show.

A turtle with shades slides on by,
Winking at a bird that forgot how to fly.
The flowers gossip, petals aflutter,
Saying, 'Last week, we spied on a nutter!'

The brook splashes with playful pride,
Flinging marshmallows, it won't let you slide.
Fairies bake cookies in the sun,
Spilling sprinkles—oh, what fun!

"Come taste our stew," the owls decree,
Made from giggles and mystery.
Join this parade of chaos and cheer,
Where every moment sings, "Stay here!"

Escapade in a Floral Reverie

Bumblebees jazz the morning light,
Buzzing like drummers, oh what a sight!
Tulips wear shades, sass on display,
"Who needs a gardener?!" They sashay.

Lemonade clouds float lazily by,
With a zesty twist and a wink to the sky.
Daisies play hopscotch with dandelions,
Chasing the wind in perfect alignments.

A picnic of giggles on soft grassy beds,
Where ants are the waiters for quirky heads.
Wild strawberries burst in a creamy swirl,
As butterflies spin in a dizzy whirl.

In this land, every joke has a punch,
Even the apples take a quirky munch.
Join the laughter, let worries be,
In this storybook realm, we're all fancy-free!

Trails of Eternal Spring

On trails where feathers fall like glitter,
Chickens hold dances, and none feel bitter.
A llama in sneakers struts down the lane,
Singing pop songs—oh, it's insane!

The sun plays hide and seek with the clouds,
While shadows shimmy, drawing funny crowds.
Squirrels recite poetry, bold and bright,
While woodchucks giggle, taking flight!

Pinecones wear jewels, oh what a thrill,
And hedgehogs offer a clumsy will.
The breeze finds us, tickling our ears,
In this land, we dissolve all our fears.

So dance to the rhythm, let laughter flow,
In the heart of this sprightly, funny show.
Every step reveals a quirk or a song,
In the charm of this journey, where we belong!

The Lure of the Silent Grove

In the grove where silence has somersaults,
Raccoons in top hats throw wobbly vaults.
A wise old tree tells riddles with a grin,
While nearby, a frog plays the violin!

Leaves whisper secrets in playful tones,
While a hedgehog dreams of ice cream cones.
A group of mushrooms share a cozy chat,
Matters of fashion, "Who wore that?"

The moon tiptoes in with a snicker,
As twilight spreads tiny stars that flicker.
Bunnies play hopscotch, gleeful and spry,
Creating a circus beneath the sky.

Here in the hush, the fun never ends,
Every twist and turn, nature bends.
Join the fray, no need for a map,
In this secret place where happiness naps!

Journey to the Luminous Grove

I strolled through trees with googly eyes,
They winked at me, what a surprise!
Squirrels danced in funny socks,
While birds were tweeting their own TikToks.

Mushrooms giggled as I walked past,
Their laughter echoed, oh so vast!
A frog in shades sang a disco tune,
Its croaks like beats under the moon.

The sun wore a hat, bright and round,
Chasing shadows all over the ground.
I tripped on laughter, fell on a vine,
Got up in style, all things aligned!

At the grove, where whimsy reigns,
I danced with flowers, embraced the gains.
Life's a riot, let the fun flow,
In this quaint place where the sillies grow.

Breezes of Tranquility

With breezes tickling my silly ears,
I tiptoed past the giggling queers.
Clouds blew kisses, fluffy and white,
While butterflies twirled left and right.

A breeze blew gently, pulling my hat,
It spun around like a playful cat.
The trees whispered secrets of pure glee,
As I stumbled along, one knee in a tree.

A dandelion puffed and started to joke,
I chuckled aloud, then it nearly broke.
Bees wore tiny rafts, splashed in a stream,
Buzzing and floating like a wild dream.

So here I sit in this topsy place,
With nature's laughter painting my face.
Breezes of whimsy, let's take a ride,
Where joy is the guide and fun's our pride.

Steps Among the Blossoms

As I tiptoed through the flowery land,
I stepped on daisies, oh wasn't it grand!
Petals giggled as they swayed and spun,
A daffodil winked at me, just for fun.

Roses in pink claimed they were cool,
While tulips told jokes like the class clown at school.
I told a pun, the lilies turned purple,
They laughed so hard, it was quite a burble.

I juggled fruit, well, gave it a try,
An apple fell down, oh my, oh my!
It rolled away, laughing all down the way,
While I chased it, all in disarray!

Peeking at bees wearing crowns made of cheese,
I gasped, then giggled at their silly tease.
Each step I take, life feels so bright,
In a land where joy takes flight.

Dawn's Embrace: A Serene Stroll

At dawn's first light, the sun had a grin,
It fluffed up the clouds, let the fun begin!
With a wink and a nod, it called out to me,
Come join this circus of jubilee!

The worms were dancing, wearing top hats,
While ants juggled crumbs, like little acrobats.
I found a snail, slow-mo in the race,
It laughed at my haste, what a funny face!

A squirrel stole my breakfast, oh what a tease,
It scampered away with the greatest of ease.
Birds cawed in laughter, like giggling friends,
In this bright new day, where silliness never ends.

So here I am, in this joyous embrace,
Chasing the giggles, a smile on my face.
Dawn breaks in laughter, let worries relent,
In this playful world where time is well spent.

Enchanted Journeys Through Green Valleys

Through fields of clover, we skip and hop,
Chasing our dreams, never wanting to stop.
Who knew that daisies could giggle so loud?
With every silly dance, we make nature proud.

The sun wears a hat, quite stylish and bright,
While clouds play hide and seek with delight.
A squirrel cracks jokes, to our sheer surprise,
We laugh till we tumble, oh how time flies!

The breeze whispers secrets, it tickles our ears,
As butterflies wink, overcoming our fears.
We trade our old worries for smiles in the air,
In this crazy garden, no reason to care.

And if the grass stains our brand new clothes,
We'll blame it on fairies and their silly shows!
With every step forward, we trip and we slide,
In this charming chaos, we cannot but glide.

Retreats Among the Cherished Groves

In the heart of the woods, we stumble and trip,
On roots like pet lizards that wiggle and flip.
A squirrel in a tutu steals all of our snacks,
We can only laugh as it winks and relax.

The trees wave their arms, like they're greeting us,
Telling old stories with a mischievous fuss.
A robin in shades breaks into a flair,
As he sings of our mischief, beyond all compare.

With mushrooms like umbrellas, we sit for a snack,
Sipping on dew drops from nature's backpack.
While ants in a row march with great ambition,
We cheer for their cause and join in their mission.

As sunbeams play tag through the branches above,
We slide down the hills, feeling light as a dove.
With each silly moment, our laughter ignites,
In this grove of delight, all is well, all feels right.

The Radiance of Untouched Petals

Amidst blooms that giggle and colors that sing,
We frolic like children, our hearts take to wing.
A bee with a bowtie joins us in fun,
As we dance on the petals, soaking up sun.

Butterflies dive-bomb, dodging our hats,
While ladybugs cheer, wearing tiny spats.
What's that in the bushes? A rabbit in disguise,
With tales of adventure and glittering eyes.

We take to the sky, on the back of a leaf,
Soaring through petals with laughter and grief.
But alas, the wind swerves, and we start to descend,
Landing in laughter with nature as friend.

We toss dandelions, wishing for flight,
But end up a-fumbling like stars in the night.
Oh, the joys that we find in this colorful spree,
Nature's a comedian, so wild and so free!

Unraveling the Magic of the Wilderness

In the wild where the laughter goes wild as the breeze,
We leap off the path, hoping not to sneeze.
With slugs in tuxedos serenading the clover,
We find our own rhythm, it's never quite over.

The trees twist and turn, like they're jiving in place,
As we twirl and we giggle, holding onto our grace.
A hedgehog with glasses gives wisdom that's sly,
As he pens old advice while we just laugh and cry.

Tales of the wild spin like whirling dervishes,
With critters that chuckle, nurturing our wishes.
From puddles of laughter to skipping through mud,
Every silly mishap turns just into fun.

So come join the ruckus, the wilderness calls,
Where every wild moment brings joy that enthralls.
With friends made of feathers and roots in the ground,
In this magical realm, pure joy can be found.

Colors of the Radiant Horizon

Balloons filled with giggles, floating high,
Dancing clouds that wave goodbye.
Sunshine spills like lemonade,
On the hills where jokes are laid.

Silly squirrels in funny hats,
Juggling acorns, look at that!
Butterflies in a comedy show,
Fluttering on tiptoes, toe to toe.

Rainbow ice cream melting fast,
Watch the drips; it's such a blast!
Laughter lines the vibrant sky,
As silly thoughts just zoom on by.

And as I stroll on this bright cue,
The world giggles; I laugh too.
Every hue, a punchline sweet,
Colors dancing beneath my feet.

Harmony in Every Step

A pogo stick beneath my shoes,
Bouncing here with silly views.
Ducks in tuxedos strut around,
Quacking jokes with every bound.

Bubbles float, a giggle spree,
Wiggly worms do the cha-cha, whee!
Llamas dressed up for a ball,
With frilly skirts, they twirl and fall.

Jumping jacks in a conga line,
Silly hats, oh, what a sign!
Footsteps echo with quirky tones,
Harmonies that tickle bones.

Every turn is a wink and grin,
In this place, joy's a win-win.
Steps may stumble, but spirits fly,
Dancing under the giggly sky.

The Enchanted Pathway

Beware of frogs with top hats on,
They'll make you laugh until you yawn.
Giggling gnomes with wands in hand,
Casting spells on the popcorn land.

Trees that sway with a silly tune,
Swaying to the light of the moon.
Marshmallow clouds, fluffy and white,
Bouncing heartbeats by day and night.

Bouncing bunnies on pogo sticks,
With carrots playing ukulele tricks.
Every step, a dance of delight,
Even shadows are giggling bright.

Follow the path where the tickles spread,
With each lolly, grin, and dread.
A whimsical ride to silly heights,
Frolicking through enchanted nights.

Whispering Willows and Serene Skies

Willows whisper with playful breeze,
Telling tales that swirl with ease.
Dancing daisies, wearing shoes,
Hop-scotch games with no excuse.

Caterpillars in sunglasses chill,
Beneath a tree atop a hill.
Sassier than the breezes light,
They spin and twirl with sheer delight.

Clouds like cotton candy swirl,
A sugary dance in a cheesy whirl.
Butterflies giggle in tandem flight,
Painting the air with vivid light.

And as I stroll between these dreams,
Nothing's ever quite as it seems.
With each step, a laugh or two,
In this sweetened world that's bright and new.

Serene Skies

Clouds shaped like puppies bounce about,
Each woof sounds like a funny shout.
Sunbeams tickle blades of grass,
While rainbows wink as they slip past.

Lollipops sprout from the ground,
Chocolate rivers that swirl around.
Silly puns riding on the breeze,
Every whisper is sure to please.

Socks with polka dots take flight,
Dancing forever in the sunny light.
Every step feels like a spree,
With giggles echoing joyfully.

Under skies of sheer delight,
Every day is a comic flight.
In this realm, we skip and sway,
Laughing as we greet the day.

Veils of Light in Hidden Sanctuaries

In a garden of giggles, where lilies play tag,
Sunflowers wear shades, what a sight, what a brag!
Bumblebees buzz with a laugh and a cheer,
While butterflies barter for nectar and beer.

A squirrel wears sneakers, races up a tree,
Challenging rabbits to join in the spree.
With each stumble and tumble, the laughter grows loud,
Even the old oak joins in, standing proud.

The daisies exchange jokes, oh what a show,
Their petals are tickled, their faces aglow.
Each blade of grass whispers secrets and glee,
While shadows waltz lightly, as if to decree.

In this hidden retreat, where silliness reigns,
Life takes on laughter, and joy breaks the chains.
Oh what a delight, in the sun's golden light,
Veils of humor and fun make everything bright!

Roaming the Heart's Haven

In a land without hurry, where clocks just won't tick,
The clouds tell tall tales, their humor quite slick.
With butterflies giggling, they flit here and there,
Playing hopscotch on rainbows, with giggles to spare.

A chubby old hedgehog lends wisdom so grand,
He polishes acorns with delicate hand.
While foxes in bowties discuss their great heists,
They're plotting sweet pranks with some mischievous mice.

Each petal's a whisper, each breeze has a joke,
The trees shake with laughter, their branches provoke.
A pond filled with giggles, the frogs croak in sync,
Making ripples of laughter, don't stop to think!

In this heart's own haven, where jesters unite,
Every moment is filled with pure, silly light.
No need for a map, just let laughter be,
Roaming this paradise, wild, joyous, and free!

Dancing Shadows on Sunlit Shores

Where shadows come alive, and flip-flops all dance,
The sand plays coy, inviting a chance.
Seagulls steal sandwiches with a cheeky squawk,
While crabs in tuxedos perform quite the walk.

The sun wears a crown, just like a disco ball,
As shells hold soirées, where sea breezes call.
Flip-flops do the cha-cha, oh what a delight,
Making waves with their rhythm, in this joyful light.

A jellyfish juggles, what a sight to behold,
While starfish share secrets, all sparkly and bold.
Each shadow takes flight, twirling 'neath the sun,
In this beachside ballet, there's laughter for fun.

So join in the frolic, let joyful hearts soar,
On shores where the shadows keep asking for more.
With each stepping wave, a giggle will pour,
Dancing in sunshine, forever adored!

A Tapestry of Pastel Hues

In a land painted sweetly, with colors that sing,
Pastel daydreams invite you to swing.
Cotton candy clouds are the thrones of delight,
While rainbows tease whispers that tickle the light.

Giggling grasshoppers throw sprinkles around,
As cheerful blue jays spread laughter profound.
A caterpillar wearing bright glasses so round,
Recites funny stories while spinning around.

The sun's a big smile, with a wink from above,
As flowers play tag, all dancing in love.
A rainbow parade is the highlight of fun,
With vivid confetti and joy on the run.

In this grand tapestry, where joy weaves anew,
Every stitch tells a tale; every hue has a clue.
So soak up the laughter, let colors imbue,
A canvas of giggles, forever in view!

Stroll Through Ethereal Meadows

In fields where daisies play and prance,
I tiptoe lightly, a clumsy dance.
Butterflies giggle, they tease and twirl,
As pollen pixies decide to swirl.

The sunbeams wink and tickle my nose,
While grasshoppers compete in a jumpy prose.
I laugh at a rabbit who wears a hat,
He's off to a tea party, imagine that!

Every cloud whispers jokes in the sky,
As shadows chase sunbeams, oh my, oh my!
I stumble upon a treasure trove,
Of jellybeans scattered, an edible grove.

The squirrels are hosting an acorn fair,
With nutty refreshments beyond compare.
I join in the fun with a skip and a hop,
But trip on a root, oh well, I won't stop!

Serenity Along Celestial Paths

Up in the clouds, I float with glee,
A burly old bear offers tea for free.
He chats about honey and mega sweet pies,
While a flock of ducks discuss fishy lies.

Passing butterflies flip, flop, and glide,
Chasing rainbows on a whimsical ride.
A ladybug tells me she's planning a race,
With ants on roller skates, oh what a place!

Each step I take is filled with delight,
As I trip on my laces – oh, what a sight!
The stars above giggle and twinkle their cheer,
While lanterns of fireflies buzz near my ear.

A mischievous wind tugs at my hat,
I shout, "Come back!" but it just flies off flat.
I laugh as I chase it, I'm caught in the spree,
In this dreamlike realm, wild and carefree!

Whispering Breezes of Bliss

The breeze tickles my ears, whispers so light,
As the squirrels take center stage for their fight.
One nut in each paw, they bicker and tease,
While a frog croaks jokes from atop a tall tree.

Clouds puff like pillows, drifting on by,
While I dance with shadows, oh me, oh my!
Each flap of my arms sends giggles around,
As the flowers giggle in their colorful gowns.

A dandelion choir bursts into song,
Inviting all critters to sing along.
The bramble bushes sway, wiggling their leaves,
While I try and fail to catch bumblebee thieves.

The sun dons sunglasses, looking quite slick,
As I try to impress with my limbo trick.
But I duck way too low, and Oops! I take a fall,
And even the daisies start laughing, that's all!

Enchanted Footsteps in Eden

Where rivers laugh and giggle with glee,
I trip on a pebble—oh, woe is me!
Silly fish wink as they flip and flop,
While I chuckle along, unable to stop.

A rainbow of colors decorates the air,
With lollipops hanging from branches up there.
I pluck one and nibble, a sugary tease,
While butterflies buzz past, whispering "Please!"

The flowers hold parades, all colors in tow,
As ants do the conga, moving in row.
I join in the fun, begin to sway wide,
Frogs ribbit applause while they hop alongside.

A breeze sways the trees, plays tag with my hair,
And I burst out in laughter, completely unaware.
As I trip on a vine, the worlds collide,
In this silly paradise, I fully abide.

Chasing Shadows Through the Glade

In the glade, shadows play,
Squirrels strut in a grand ballet.
A mushroom wears a tiny hat,
While crickets sing to a party rat.

Butterflies sip on nectar sweet,
Bouncing around on nimble feet.
A bunny dons a monocle fine,
Claiming picnic spots like it's divine.

Trees gossip while winds confide,
Leaves laugh as they take a ride.
Hiding behind the bushes' embrace,
Chasing the laughter, we join the race.

In this merry, whimsical glade,
Who knew nature could throw such a charade?
Tickled by breeze and playful cheer,
Shadows mingle as we disappear.

Serendipity in Blooming Vistas

In bloom, the flowers play dress-up,
Petals giggle, sipping from a cup.
A bee's wearing sunglasses so bright,
Buzzing lyrics, in pure delight.

The daisies wear skirts, swaying near,
Tickled by winds, they twirl with cheer.
A snail glides by wearing a crown,
Declaring himself the king of the town.

Colorful chaos in the bright sun's care,
Butterflies dance without a single care.
Sipping dew as if on a spree,
Nature's humor is wild and free.

Fields alive with blossoms so bold,
Their laughter fills the air, uncontrolled.
Serendipity winks, and we cheer,
In this silly paradise, nothing to fear.

Dancing with the Midnight Breeze

When night falls, the stars come out,
Whispers of mischief, they twist and shout.
Moonbeams jive with shadows' groove,
Swaying together, they're in the mood.

Fireflies flaunt their tiny lights,
Winking, giggling, in crazy flights.
A raccoon leads a conga line,
Hats off to the moon - what a sign!

Suddenly, owls drop their wise act,
Fluffing their feathers - what a pact!
A night of antics through bright trees,
Sippin' on mischief with the midnight breeze.

With laughter echoing, we join this spree,
Jumping over dreams, wild and free.
In this realm where the oddities tease,
Who knew nature could throw such a tease?

Meadows of Radiant Stillness

In the meadow, silence wears a grin,
Grasshoppers debate whose turn to spin.
A dandelion, with mischief in tow,
Puffs its cheeks, letting wishes flow.

Quiet moments hold a cheeky giggle,
The old oak tree gives a hearty wiggle.
A lone worm waves, slick and bold,
Claiming he's a knight, proud and gold.

Dewdrops bounce like marbles, it's true,
Each holding secrets, shiny and new.
Sunbeams peek through leaves just to tease,
While the wildflowers sway with such ease.

In the stillness, whispers flutter and swirl,
Nature's humor, a joyful whirl.
These meadows invite us to play and freeze,
A comedic refuge, a moment to seize.

Serenading Streams Under Moonlit Canopies

Beneath the trees, the critters play,
A raccoon strums a branch all day.
Frogs croak tunes in a bubbly band,
While fireflies dance, a glowing hand.

A squirrel joins with a tiny jig,
The moonlight shines, it's all quite big.
I laugh aloud at their wild prance,
These woodland folks, a nightly dance.

I tripped on roots and laughed so free,
Who knew the tree was out to tease?
With splashes bright in streams below,
I'm soaked and smiling, what a show!

So gather 'round for tunes tonight,
Nature's band plays till morning light.
With heart afire, I'd not decline,
To sway with critters, so divine.

Embraced by Earth's Gentle Caress

In fields of green, a tumble I take,
With daisies dancing, my nose does shake.
A bumblebee buzzes, declares its reign,
While chasing butterflies, I feel no pain.

Clouds roll in with a friendly poke,
Saying, 'Hey you, don't choke on the smoke!'
I laugh with the wind, as it tugs my hat,
A merry chase, oh, just like that!

With mud on my shoes and grass in my hair,
I strike a pose, like I just don't care.
The sun winks down at my goofy grin,
Started with joy; I'm not sure where to begin!

In this wild space, all worries pause,
As I spin and twirl, forgetting the cause.
Happiness blooms in each clumsy step,
Embraced by nature; oh, my heart leapt!

Traces of Joy in Dappled Glades

In glades of sunlight, shadows play,
I stomp on leaves that crunch away.
A rabbit darts with a cheeky hop,
    Chasing it, I cannot stop!

Dappled light spills like warm peach tea,
I land in a patch, all giggles and glee.
With butterflies laughing in chorus, loud,
    I'm the king of this silly crowd!

I made a crown with twigs and leaves,
Twisting up laughter; oh, how it weaves!
With ladybugs as my royal guards,
I toast with dew on a bed of yards!

The sun begins its slow descent,
But my happiness is heaven-sent.
In playful mirth, I say goodnight,
To my dappled friends, oh what a sight!

The Allure of Timeless Trails

On winding paths, where the whispers live,
A wobbly bear shares all that it can give.
Hiccups of laughter echo around,
As I trip over roots, the ground I found!

With every twist, a new riddle appears,
The trees lean close, as if to share cheers.
While squirrels chuckle from branches up high,
At my graceful pirouette; oh my, oh my!

The daisies conspire in colors so bright,
They poke out their heads, an amusing sight.
With the softest tickles from blades at my feet,
I lose track of time amidst nature's beat.

Each trail tells tales with a giggle or two,
In this quirky realm, all dreams come true.
With muddy paws and a heart full of mirth,
I dance through the world, oh what a birth!

The Glistening Embrace of Light

Sunshine sneezes, the rays take flight,
Bouncing off flowers, a dazzling sight.
Bees wear sunglasses, buzzing in style,
They dance in circles, all the while.

The pond reflects a winking smile,
Frogs in tuxedos, croaking with style.
A fish does a flip, takes a bow with grace,
While ducks quack jokes, in this sunny place.

Laughter floats high on warm, breezy air,
A squirrel's rubber band shoots without care.
Chasing his acorn, he rolls down the hill,
With every tumble, the world stands still.

Last one to splash is a brown, fuzzy cat,
Who promptly runs off, wearing a hat.
In this shimmering realm, where silliness gleams,
Every tiny creature chases their dreams.

Hushed Melodies of the Meadow

In a field of clovers, the feathers of birds,
Whisper sweet secrets, tucked in their words.
A snail takes a selfie, a worm rolls his eyes,
As daisies debate who has the best ties.

The breeze plays a tune, on the flutes of the grass,
While ants rehearse for their next bug class.
A butterfly grins, sending winks to the crowd,
As ladybugs clap, all cheerful and loud.

A turtle's slow dance, leaves others confused,
While grasshoppers talk, they seem rather fused.
With mischief afoot, and laughter galore,
The meadow hums tunes, we can't help but adore.

While clouds drift above, like cotton in flight,
The sun starts to yawn, it's almost bedtime light.
Yet mischief continues, as stars start to peek,
In this hush of the meadow, you've nothing to seek.

Heartbeats of the Evergreen Lands

In forests of green, there's a rhythm so bright,
The owls are beatboxing, what a strange sight!
A bear's doing yoga, stretched under a tree,
While chipmunks sing duets, up high and so free.

Pine cones roll by, competing with glee,
Creating a race, on a squirrel's decree.
A stream cracks a joke, rocks chuckle and sway,
While ferns hold their bellies, and giggle away.

The wind whispers tales, and tickles the pines,
A fox in a fedora, looks quite divine.
Grumpy old trees, ramble on nightly,
While blossoms debate, who's blooming most brightly.

But wait! Here comes trouble, a deer with a bow,
Carrying bagpipes, in a jolly show.
As laughter erupts in this evergreen glade,
Nature's gathering plays, their plans never fade.

Enchanted Landmarks of Wonder

A rainbow stretched out, like a slip-and-slide,
While clouds play hopscotch, oh what a ride!
A castle of waffles, towers of cream,
Where syrup falls gently, in a sweet dream.

The hills roll with laughter, tickling the sky,
While marshmallow mountains wave bye-bye.
Unicorns sketch plans, for a picnic spree,
While jellybean rivers sing songs of glee.

Here trees wear hats, with a smile so wide,
And critters in carriages take a fun ride.
Candy canes twirl, in a glorious dance,
As gummy bears gossip, in their sweet trance.

As stars pop like popcorn, in the evening grand,
The moon joins the party, at the critters' command.
In this land of wonder, where silliness reigns,
Every corner invites you to join in the chains.

Dreamy Trails Beneath Shimmering Skies

With sandals on, I trip and sway,
The butterflies laugh as I dance away.
A squirrel steals my snack with glee,
While I chase it, almost on one knee.

Clouds above like fluffy sheep,
I stare and imagine them counting me deep.
A bird drops a message, right on my hat,
Thanks for the gift, but I'd rather not chat!

Flowers wink, they're in on the joke,
Dandelions giggle as I choke on smoke.
The breeze, it nudges, gives me a shove,
"Keep moving, silly, you've misplaced your love!"

At sunset, I trip on a root once more,
The trees seem to giggle, what's behind that door?
Every stumble, a laugh, a splendid delight,
Oh, how I cherish this goofy night!

Wandering Where Sunlight Lingers

I skip and pout, a feisty little sprite,
The sun plays peek-a-boo, what a funny sight!
Grass tickles my feet, oh, what a prank,
While shadows dance near, they play with my flank.

Chasing my hat as it flies in the breeze,
A leaf sweeps in, giggling through trees.
Who knew serenity could be this absurd?
I giggle at clouds that look like a bird.

A picnic awaits with ants on parade,
They're marching for crumbs, I'm not quite dismayed.
The lemonade spills, oh what a blunder!
"Do ants love a party?" I ponder in wonder.

With the moon now peeking as if it's a guest,
I trip on my words, but I smile with zest.
In this light-hearted stroll, I'm never alone,
Life's just a stage, and I'm in the zone!

Journey of Tranquil Echoes

Whispers of echo, I hear a chime,
A squirrel serenades, oh, isn't it prime?
Each step rolls out laughs, my toes give a shout,
Nature's my witness, without any doubt.

I meet a wise owl sporting a hat,
He winks as he says, "Mind the dog with a spat!"
Twirling around, I accidentally fall,
Bouncing on petals, my giggle's a call.

Under the leaves, a party's in tow,
The insects are dancing, they put on a show.
My shoe's not the size of a small little bug,
But they all offer me a cozy warm hug.

As twilight arrives, the fireflies spark,
I trip over laughter, oh, what a lark!
In this dance of joy, I twirl and I soar,
Life is a circus, who could ask for more?

Lush Lullabies of Nature

In the garden, I'm twirling, my head in a daze,
The flowers are up to mischief, what a wild maze!
With sun on my cheeks and bees above head,
I giggle at daisies scheming in red.

A toad croaks a tune, so offbeat and bold,
I bow to the rhythm, watch it unfold.
Butterflies flit by like they're in a race,
While I duck and weave at an awkward pace.

Puddles splash stories of mischief and fun,
Each leap tells a tale of adventures begun.
The sky throws a wink, it's a quirky affair,
With cloud-shaped llamas floating in air.

As stars fill the sky, I wave them goodnight,
Thankful for giggles in this magical light.
In this playful realm, I'll always belong,
Forever the fool, my heart sings a song!

www.ingramcontent.com/pod-product-compliance
Lightning Source LLC
Chambersburg PA
CBHW072123070526
44585CB00016B/1541